Weights
and Measures

Library Edition Published 1991

Published by Marshall Cavendish Corporation
2415 Jerusalem Avenue
PO Box 587, North Bellmore,
N.Y. 11710
Library edition produced by Pemberton Press

Printed in Italy by New Interlitho, Milan

© Marshall Cavendish Corporation 1991
© Cherrytree Press Ltd. 1990

Library of Congress Cataloging in-Publication Data

Karrod, Robin.
    Weights and measures / by Robin Kerrod and Susan Baker:
illustrated by Mike Atkinson.
        p. cm. – (Secrets of Science)
    Includes index.
    Summary: Explains the origins of weights and measures. How they
have changed over the years, and how they can be used to measure
different things. Includes projects and questions
        ISBN 1-85435-269-5 (lib. bdg.).
    1. Weights and Measures – Juvenile literature. (1. Weights and
Measures.) I. Baker, Susan. II. Atkinson, Mike, II. II. Title,
IV. Series: Kerrod, Robin. Secrets of Science
QC90.6.K47 1991
630.0 – dc20   80-25570
                                                      CIP
                                                       AC

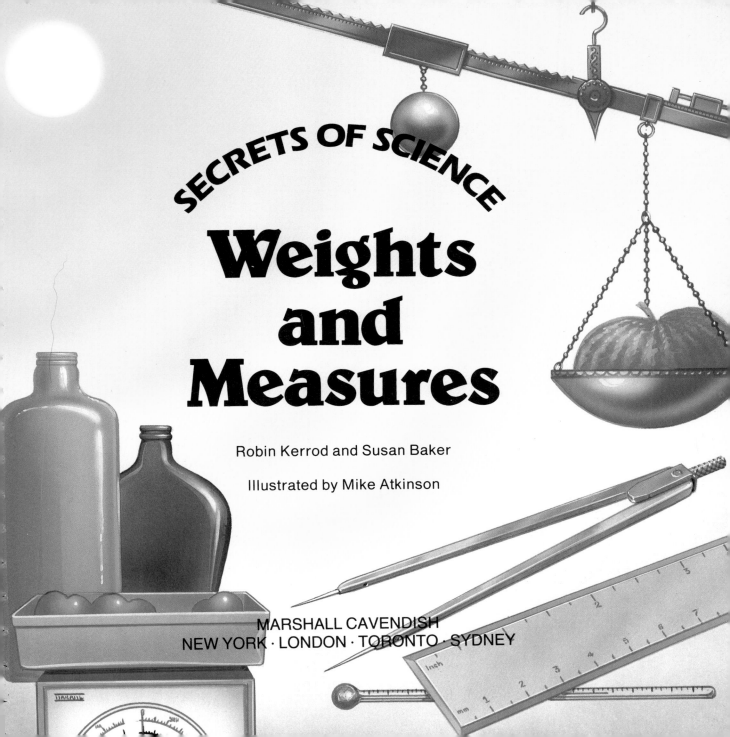

SECRETS OF SCIENCE

Weights and Measures

Robin Kerrod and Susan Baker

Illustrated by Mike Atkinson

MARSHALL CAVENDISH
NEW YORK · LONDON · TORONTO · SYDNEY

Safety First

☐ Ask your parents or another adult for permission before you start any experiment, especially if you are using matches or anything hot, sharp, or poisonous.

☐ Wear old clothes, or cover your clothes with an old shirt or apron.

☐ If you work on a table, use an old one and protect it with paper or cardboard.

☐ Do water experiments in the sink or outdoors.

☐ Strike matches away from your body, and make sure they are out before you throw them away.

☐ Make sure candles are standing securely.

☐ Wear oven gloves when handling anything hot.

☐ Take care when cutting things. Always cut away from your body.

☐ Don't use cans with jagged edges. Use ones with lids.

☐ Use only non-toxic white glue, glue sticks, or paste.

☐ Never taste chemicals, unless the book tells you to.

☐ Label all bottles and jars containing chemicals, and store them where young children can't get at them – and not in the family food cupboard.

☐ Never use or play with household electricity. It can KILL. Use a flashlight or dry cell.

☐ When you have finished an experiment, put your things away, clean up, and wash your hands.

Contents

Measuring Up

We need to make measurements all the time. Can you reach the top shelf? Is the box too heavy to lift? Is there enough flour left to make a cake? Is there time to bake it before dinner? Can you wear last year's coat or have you grown too tall or too fat?

Often we guess the length, size, and weight of things. Sometimes we need to know exact measurements. When you build a model, the parts will not fit unless they are measured correctly. When you buy candy, you want to know that you are getting the right amount for your money.

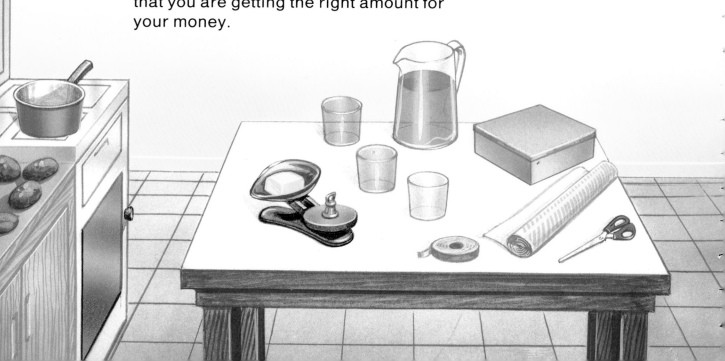

Look at the pictures and see if you can answer the questions. Look around the room you are in and ask similar questions. If you want exact answers you will need something to measure with. Things you measure with are called measures or measuring instruments. A ruler is a measuring instrument. So is a clock.

Measuring Questions

1 Is the pan big enough to hold the potatoes?

2 Should there be more or less butter in the scale to balance the weight?

3 Is there enough juice in the pitcher to fill all the glasses?

4 Is the wrapping paper wide enough to cover the box?

5 Is there enough tape left on the roll?

6 Look at the clock. How long is it until bedtime?

7 Which is running faster, the dog or the cat?

8 Is the shade long enough to cover the window? How much farther must it be pulled?

9 Is the sun too hot for the plants on the window?

Rule of Thumb

Long ago, people used parts of their bodies as measures. They compared small lengths with the size of their hands or fingers. Use your thumb as a measure. How many thumbs tall is this book?

The ancient Egyptians called the distance from a man's elbow to the tip of his middle finger a cubit. They called their outspread fingers a span. Two spans made one cubit. Are two spans of your hand as long as your forearm?

Egyptian Measures

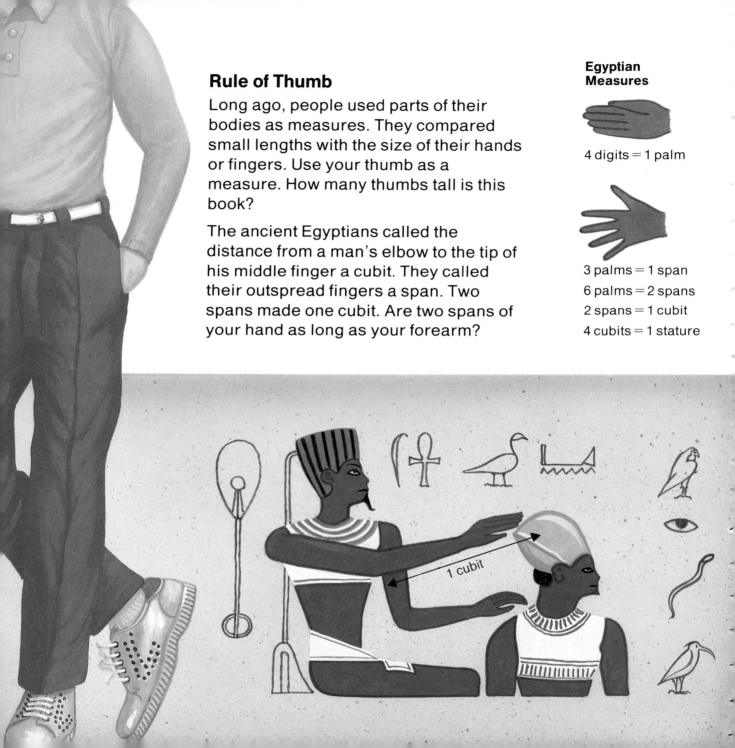

4 digits = 1 palm

3 palms = 1 span
6 palms = 2 spans
2 spans = 1 cubit
4 cubits = 1 stature

1 cubit

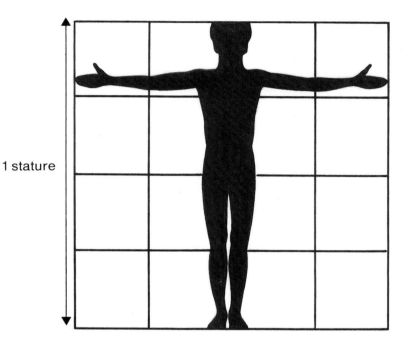

1 stature

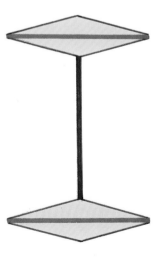

Long, Short, and Right Sight

1 Is your thumb exactly the same size as the person's sitting next to you? Measure them and see. We often need to measure things more accurately than with our thumbs or by guessing. Use a ruler for this experiment.

2 Look at the picture on the left. Is the brown line down the middle longer than the red lines inside the diamonds? Are both red lines the same length? Guess first, then measure the lines with a ruler.

3 Look at the three matchsticks on the right. Which one is the longest? Measure the one you think is longest, then measure the other two.

4 Get your friends to guess. You can bet they will not be right unless they measure.

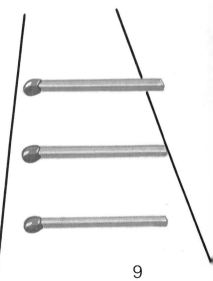

9

Whose Feet?

The Romans used the uncia, which was the width of a thumb, to measure things. We get our word inch from uncia. Twelve uncia was roughly equal to the length of a man's foot.

Roman soldiers went on long marches. They paced out the distances. A pace is two strides, one with the left foot and one with the right. One pace measured five feet. Mark out the distance you travel in two strides. See how many feet long your pace is.

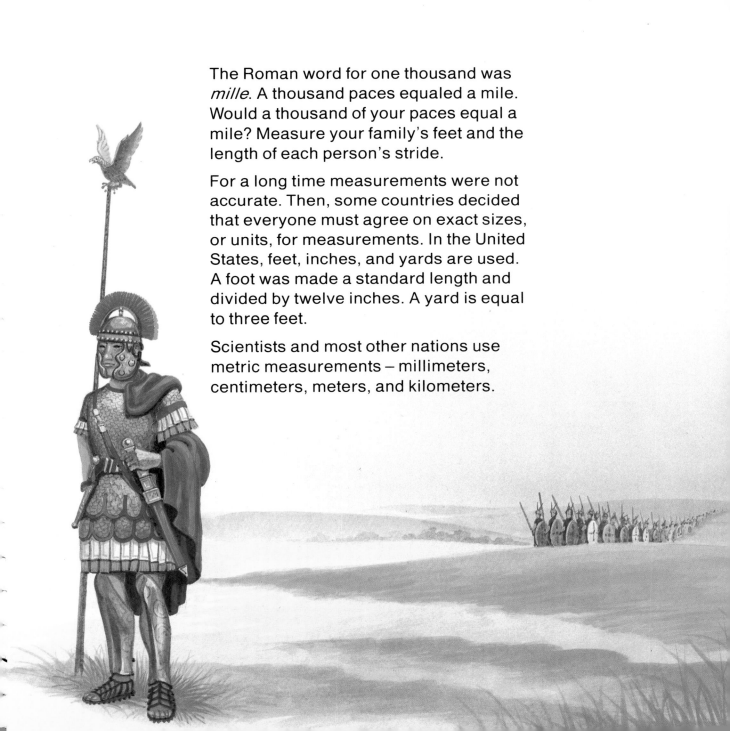

The Roman word for one thousand was *mille*. A thousand paces equaled a mile. Would a thousand of your paces equal a mile? Measure your family's feet and the length of each person's stride.

For a long time measurements were not accurate. Then, some countries decided that everyone must agree on exact sizes, or units, for measurements. In the United States, feet, inches, and yards are used. A foot was made a standard length and divided by twelve inches. A yard is equal to three feet.

Scientists and most other nations use metric measurements – millimeters, centimeters, meters, and kilometers.

Tipping the Balance

Hold a baseball mitt in one hand and a ball in the other. Which feels heavier? The ancient Egyptians compared the weights of stone or metal with the things they bought. A one-pound weight was equal to the weight of 70,000 grains of ripe wheat. It was much easier to weigh the grains than to count them!

The Egyptians weighed their grain in balancing scales. A balance was two hanging pans. When the weights of the pans are equal the scales balance exactly. If one side is heavier, it tips the balance.

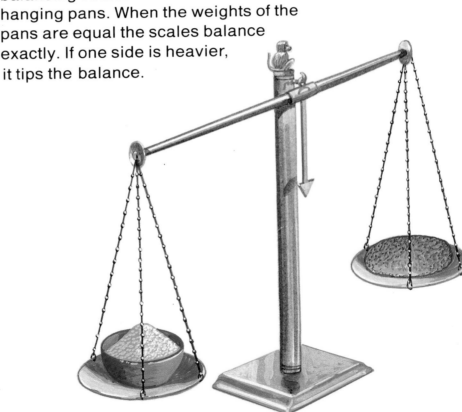

Make Balancing Scales

1 You need a coat hanger, two identical paper cups, two lengths of string, some tape, a thin stick or knitting needle to act as a pointer, and a piece of paper.

2 Hang the hanger on a hook and tape the pointer to its center.

3 Stick the paper to the wall behind the pointer. Mark a vertical line on the paper where the pointer hangs. Then mark vertical lines to the left and right of it.

4 Attach a length of string to each of the cups to make a handle. Each handle must be exactly the same length.

5 Hang the cups on the hanger and make sure that they hang level. The pointer should be on the vertical line.

6 Now use your scales to compare the weights of things. Use marbles in one cup to compare the weight of things in the other. Weigh sand, water, small toys, rice, dried beans, etc.

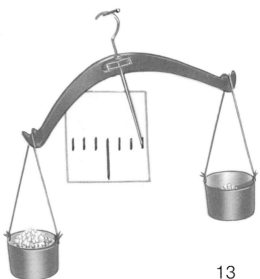

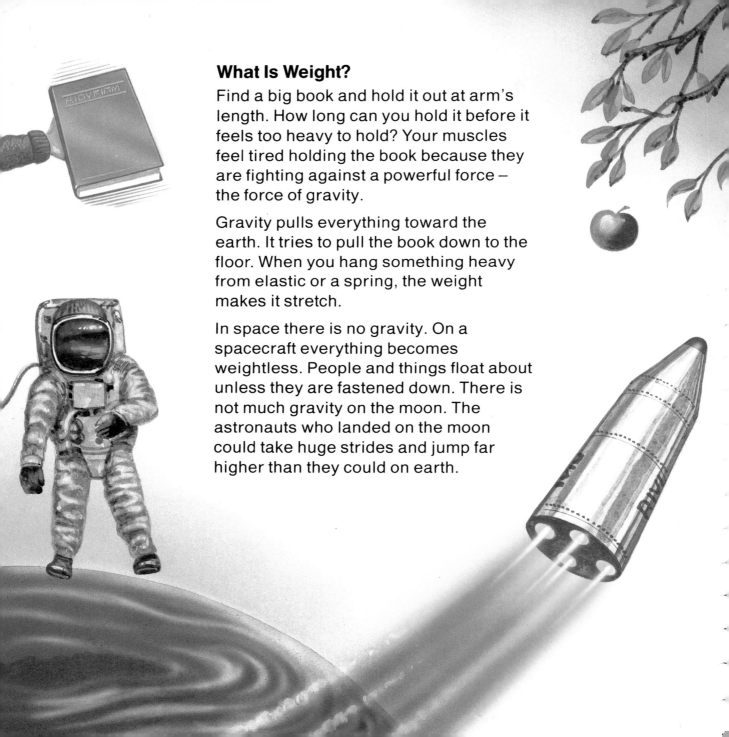

What Is Weight?

Find a big book and hold it out at arm's length. How long can you hold it before it feels too heavy to hold? Your muscles feel tired holding the book because they are fighting against a powerful force – the force of gravity.

Gravity pulls everything toward the earth. It tries to pull the book down to the floor. When you hang something heavy from elastic or a spring, the weight makes it stretch.

In space there is no gravity. On a spacecraft everything becomes weightless. People and things float about unless they are fastened down. There is not much gravity on the moon. The astronauts who landed on the moon could take huge strides and jump far higher than they could on earth.

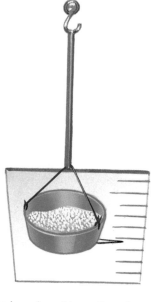
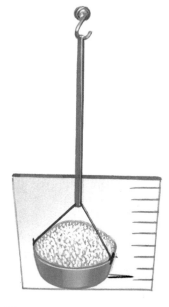

Make a Spring Balance

1 You need a small plastic container, paper, tape, a toothpick to make a pointer, a rubber band, and some string or twine.

2 Hang the rubber band from a hook.

3 Thread the twine through the band and tape it to the container to make a handle.

4 Tape the pointer to the bottom of the container so that it sticks out at the side.

5 Put the paper behind the container when it is hanging empty. Make a mark where the pointer rests. Mark a scale below it.

6 Now weigh things in the container. See how much each weight causes the rubber band to stretch. If you double the weight, the band should stretch twice as much.

Make Bathroom Scales

1 You need a bed spring, a can with a lid that will hold the coiled spring, a pointer, and tape.

2 Put the spring into the can, and mark a scale on it.

3 Put a lid on the spring, and sit weights on top of it. Mark the level the lid sinks to.

Types of Scales

bathroom scale

spring scale

balance scale

modern electronic scale

U.S. Weights and Measures

Eight hundred years ago, King Henry I of England decided that everyone must use one measuring system. The system became known as the English system. It was similar to the Roman system of miles, feet and inches.

Today this system is used in the United States and some other countries.

Length

12 inches = 1 foot
3 feet = 1 yard
1,760 yards = 1 mile

Weight

16 ounces = 1 pound
1 ton = 2,000 pounds

inches

16

Metric Weights and Measures

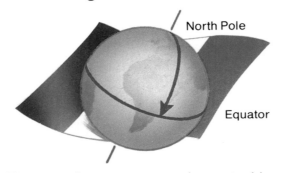

North Pole

Equator

The metric system was invented in France. It is based on the size of the earth. The distance between the North Pole and the equator is divided into 10 million equal parts. Each one is a meter.

Length

10 millimeters = 1 centimeter
100 centimeters = 1 meter
1,000 meters = 1 kilometer

Weight

1,000 milligrams = 1 gram
1,000 grams = 1 kilogram
1,000 kilograms = 1 metric ton

Why do you think the metric system is easier to use than the U.S. system?

Measuring Length

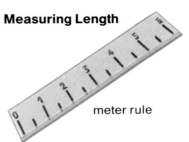

meter rule

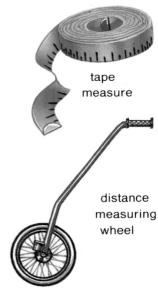

tape measure

distance measuring wheel

car odometer

centimeters

17

sundial

Timing Time

Long ago, people got up when it was light and went to bed when it was dark. People told the time by the position of the sun in the sky. At noon the sun is overhead. Sundials use the sun's shadow to show the time of day.

Then people invented ways of measuring time when it was not sunny.

water clock

candle clock

hourglass

The sand in an hourglass takes exactly one hour to run from one bulb of the glass to the other.

Water drains slowly out of a water clock to show how much time has passed.

As the wax burns away, the marks on a candle clock gradually disappear.

1 hour

2 hours

3 hours

pendulum clock

clock workings

Make a Candle Clock

1 You need two candles, a waterproof marker, a watch or clock, some matches and an adult to help.

2 Stick the two candles into holders side by side, but not too close together. You can stick them on saucers, but make sure that they are stuck firmly.

3 Light one of the candles and look at your watch. Wait until an hour (or ½ hour) has passed. At the exact second, mark the unlit candle level with the lit one.

4 Now wait another hour and make a second mark. Carry on until the first candle has burned away. Now you can mark any other candles that you have. Could you mark the half and quarter hours on the candles?

digital watch

digital clock

stop watch

Clocks measure time more accurately. In old clocks, a pendulum swung back and forth each second. It was attached to a set of gears and wheels. They moved the hands of the clock to show the time.

Modern clocks and watches contain microchips with computer circuits on them. They count electrical impulses that mark fractions of a second. They show the time as figures of light. They are called digital clocks or watches.

Hot or Cold?

The hotness or coldness of something is called its temperature. See if you can tell the temperature of a bowl of water with this experiment.

The Water Test

1 You need three bowls, some cold water, and some water that is hot but not too hot to put your hands in.

2 Fill one bowl with hot water and one bowl with cold water. Fill the third bowl with a mixture of the two so that it is lukewarm.

3 Put one hand in the cold bowl and one hand in the hot bowl for a little while. Then, put both hands in the third bowl. Is the water hot or cold?

To tell the temperature we use a thermometer. A thermometer is a glass tube with a scale on it. It has liquid inside it. Liquids expand when they are hot. When the temperature rises, the liquid inside the thermometer expands and goes up the tube.

thermometer

There are two scales for measuring temperature. The system used in the United States is named Fahrenheit after the man who invented it. On his scale, the freezing point of water is at 32°F and the boiling point is 212°F.

The other system is called the Celcius, or centigrade, scale. On this scale 0°C is the point at which water freezed. The point at which water boils is 100°C.

greenhouse thermometer

clinical thermometer

Your body has its own normal temperature. It is about 98.6°F (37°C). When you are ill your temperature goes up. Doctors measure your temperature with a clinical thermometer. Gardeners use thermometers to see when it is getting too hot or cold for their plants.

Ovens, irons, and other gadgets control their temperature with an instrument called a thermostat. When the temperature gets too hot, the thermostat turns off the electricity. When it cools, it switches it back on.

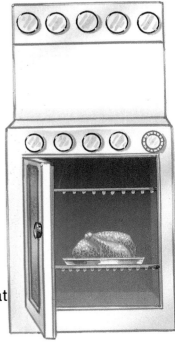

Faster and Faster

How fast can you run? To work out your speed, divide the distance you run by the time it takes. Get a friend to time you with a stopwatch or a watch that shows seconds as well as minutes.

To measure the distance, you can use a bicycle. First, make a clear mark on the wheel. Measure the distance right around the wheel. Then, wheel the bike over your running track. Start with the mark on the ground.

Watch the mark, and count how many times it hits the ground as the wheel turns. Multiply the number of turns by the size of the wheel to work out the length of the track.

Once you know the length of the track, you can get on your bike and measure your cycling speed.

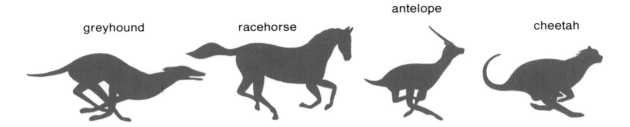

greyhound   racehorse   antelope   cheetah

A cheetah can reach its top speed faster than an antelope, a racehorse, and a greyhound. But even a cheetah takes time to build up speed. It cannot go from a standstill to its top speed in an instant. Slowing down to a stop takes time, too.

When something increases speed, it accelerates. Drivers press a pedal to make their cars accelerate. You can see the needle on the speedometer move around as the car builds up speed. The brakes make the car slow down, or decelerate.

speedometer

Making an Impression

Next time you are at the beach try this experiment. Walk across the sand in a pair of boots. Then, borrow some high heels and try walking in them. What do you think would happen if you tried it?

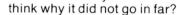

Nail It!

1 You need a hammer and two nails, a block of wood, and an adult to help.

2 Hammer one nail into a piece of wood. Hit it on the head.

3 Turn the other nail upside down and hammer that into the wood. Be very careful!

4 Did the second nail sink in as far as the first nail? Did you hit it as hard? Can you think why it did not go in far?

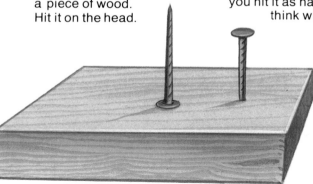

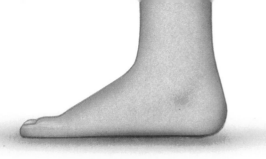

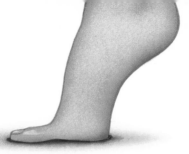

If you stand on damp sand, your feet leave a small dent in the sand. If you stand on tiptoes, your toes sink right in. You have halved the area your weight is spread over. You have made the pressure twice as great. It is just like the hammer and the nail.

There is pressure all around us. We cannot feel the weight of the air but it presses down on us all the same. Water presses down, too. Deep-sea divers have to wear strong metal suits. The armor stops the weight of the water crushing their bodies.

Water Pressure

1 You need an old plastic container, something to make holes with, and some water.

2 Make a line of holes up the side of the container.

3 Fill the container with water and stand it at the edge of the sink or outdoors.

4 Watch the little fountains spurt through the holes. Which hole has the weakest jet? What happens to the jets as the water level drops?

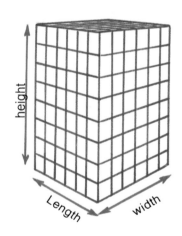

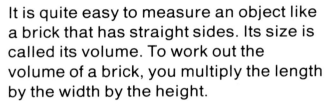

What is the area of this rectangle?

Area and Volume

The size of a surface is called its area. A surface with four sides is called a rectangle. It is easy to work out the area of a rectangle. You multiply the length by the width.

Not all surfaces have straight sides. A good way to work out areas that do not have straight sides is to divide them into squares. Then, you can count the whole squares and add on the halves and quarters.

It is quite easy to measure an object like a brick that has straight sides. Its size is called its volume. To work out the volume of a brick, you multiply the length by the width by the height.

It is much more difficult to measure the volume of a pile of apples. The trick is to use water. When an object sinks in water, it pushes some of the water out of the way to make space for itself. It displaces the water. The size, or volume, of the object is equal to the amount of water it displaces.

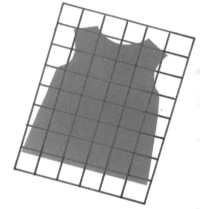

What is the area of this dress pattern?

What is the volume of this cube?

How would you measure these apples?

26

The Water Trick

1 You need a plastic cup, a bowl to sit the cup in, some water, some small objects to measure, and a measuring cup.

2 Fill the cup to the brim with water. Take an odd-shaped object, and drop it into the water.

3 See how much water spills out of the cup as the object sinks. Measure the displaced water in a measuring cup.

4 The volume of water that overflows equals the volume of the object that displaces it.

Check your experiment with an even-shaped object like a brick. First, measure it with a tape measure, then measure it using the water method.

Guess the Volume

1 You need bottles of all different sizes and shapes and some water.

2 Line your bottles up in order of size.

3 Fill up the one you think holds the most.

4 Pour water from that one into the next one. Then, pour water from that one into the next, and so on.

5 If you guessed right, you should end up with a little water in each bottle.

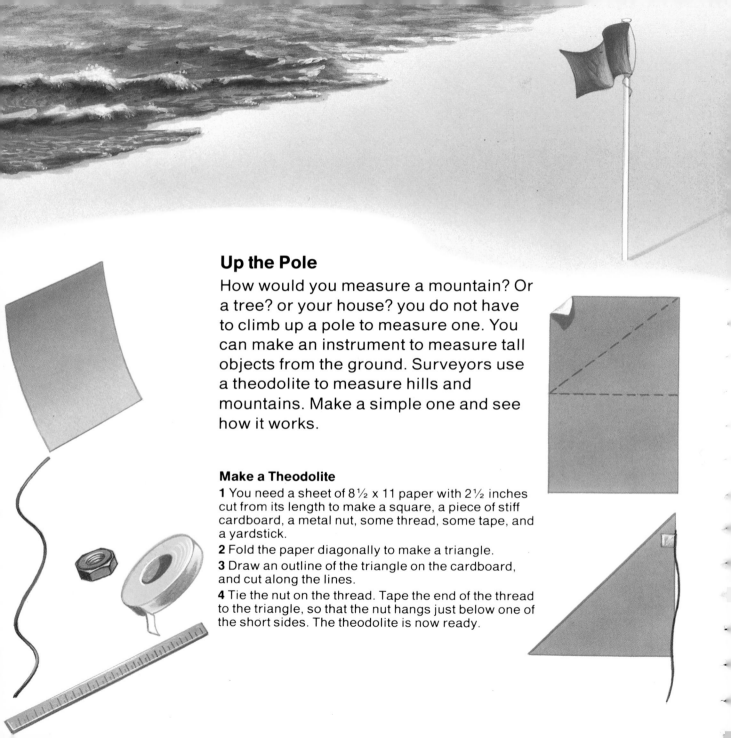

Up the Pole

How would you measure a mountain? Or a tree? or your house? you do not have to climb up a pole to measure one. You can make an instrument to measure tall objects from the ground. Surveyors use a theodolite to measure hills and mountains. Make a simple one and see how it works.

Make a Theodolite

1 You need a sheet of 8½ x 11 paper with 2½ inches cut from its length to make a square, a piece of stiff cardboard, a metal nut, some thread, some tape, and a yardstick.

2 Fold the paper diagonally to make a triangle.

3 Draw an outline of the triangle on the cardboard, and cut along the lines.

4 Tie the nut on the thread. Tape the end of the thread to the triangle, so that the nut hangs just below one of the short sides. The theodolite is now ready.

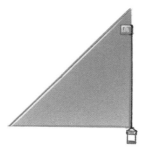

5 To measure a tree or flagpole, hold the triangle up to your eye so that you are looking along the long edge. Make sure that the thread hangs straight down the far edge.

6 Looking toward the pole, walk forward or backward (be careful) until the top of the pole is in line with the tip of the triangle.

7 Mark where you are standing. Then measure the distance to the bottom of the pole with the yardstick.

8 The height of the pole is that distance plus your own height.

Conversion Tables

It is easy to convert measurements from one measuring system to another. Use a calculator to help you multiply. The figures you need are in the tables. To convert measurements to metric, multiply by the figures on the right.

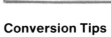

Metric to U.S.

Weight
1 gram = 0.035 ounces
1 kilogram = 2.2 pounds
1 metric ton = 2,204 pounds

Length
1 centimeter = 0.39 inch
1 meter = 39.37 inches
1 kilometer = 0.62 mile

Area
1 square centimeter = 0.155 square inch
1 square meter = 1,550 square inches
1 square kilometer = 0.386 square mile

Volume
1 cubic centimeter = 0.061 cubic inch
1 cubic meter = 35.31 cubic feet

Capacity 1 liter = 2.1 pints or 0.26 gallon

Temperature
$1°C = 9/5°F$
To convert °C to °F, multiply by 9/5 and add 32.

Conversion Tips
● Some bathroom and kitchen scales include metric measurements on them. You can change pounds to kilograms at a glance.
● Cars have miles and kilometers on their speedometers. If you are going at 100 kilometers per hour, how many miles per hour are you doing? Look at the dial to find the answer.

To convert metric to U.S. measurements, multiply by the figures on the right.

Whenever you measure something, practice converting it to the other system.

250 grams of butter weighs about ½ pound.

2 pounds of sugar weighs about 1 kilo.

1 liter of juice is just over 2 pints.

4 liters of oil is just over 1 gallon.

● You can convert liquid measurements by reading the scales on a measuring cup. Check that the scale is accurate with a calculator.

U.S. to Metric

Weight
1 ounce = 28.3 gram
1 pound = 453.6 grams
1 ton = 0.9 metric ton

Length
1 inch = 2.54 centimeters
1 foot = 30.48 centimeters
1 mile = 1.61 kilometers

Area
1 square inch = 6.45 square centimeters
1 square foot = 0.093 square meters
1 square mile = 2.59 square kilometers

Volume
1 cubic inch = 16.39 cubic centimeters
1 cubic foot = 0.028 cubic meters

Capacity
1 pint = 0.47 liter (0.57 UK liter) 1 gallon = 3.8 liters (4.5 UK liter)

Temperature
$1°F = 5/9°C$
to convert °F to °C, subtract 32 and multiply by 5/9.

Index and glossary

acceleration 23 *the rate at which speed increases; an accelerating body travels faster and faster*
area 26
a measure of the amount of surface an object has

balance 12, 13
an instrument on which an object is weighed by being balanced by weights of known value
bathroom scales 15

candle clock 18, 19
a candle marked with a scale, which tells the time as it burns down
Celsius 21
the scale of temperature, named after the Swedish scientist Anders Celsius. Water freezes at 0 degrees Celsius (0°C) and boils at 100°C.
centigrade 21
an alternative name for the Celsius scale
centimeter 11, 17
one-hundredth of a meter
clock 7, 18, 19
a device or instrument for telling the time
cubit 8

deceleration 23
the opposite of acceleration; the rate at which an object slows down
degrees 21
the units on a temperature scale; or the units in which angles are measured
digital clock 19
a clock that displays the time by numbers, or digits
digital watch 19
a watch that displays the time by numbers, or digits

Fahrenheit 21
a scale of temperature named after the German scientist Gabriel Fahrenheit; water freezes at 32 degrees Fahrenheit (32°F) and boils at 212°F
foot 10, 11, 16

gram 17
one-thousandth of a kilogram
gravity 14
the pull of the earth, which gives objects their weight

hour 18, 19

hourglass 18
a device that uses trickling sand to measure time

inch 10, 11, 16

kilogram 17
the standard unit of weight in the metric system
kilometer 17

meter 11, 17
metric system 11, 17, 30, 31
a system of weights and measures, based on the meter for measuring length and the kilogram for measuring weight
Metric ton 17
1,000 kilograms

mile 11, 16

millimeter 11, 17
one-thousandth of a meter

ounce 16

pound 12, 16
pressure 25
the force pressing down over a certain area

ruler 7

scales 12, 15
speed 22, 23
a measure of the distance an object travels in a certain time
spring balance 15
stop watch 19, 22
sundial 18
a device that tells the time by the position of a shadow

temperature 20, 21
a measure of how hot a body is
theodolite 28
an instrument that measures angles
thermometer 20, 21
an instrument that measures temperature
thermostat 21
a device that keeps something at a steady temperature
time 7, 18, 19
ton 16
2,000 pounds

U.S. system 16, 17, 30, 31
the system of weights and measures used in the U.S.

volume 26, 27
a measure of the space something occupies

watch 19
weight 12, 13, 14
the downward force an object exerts because of gravity

yard 11, 16
yardstick 28, 29